FAMOUS PEOPLE
FAMOUS LIVES

Biographies of famous people to
support the curriculum.

Henry Ford

by Peter Kent
Illustrations by Peter Kent

FRANKLIN WATTS
NEW YORK • LONDON • SYDNEY

First published in 1999 by
Franklin Watts
96 Leonard Street
London
EC2A 4XD

Franklin Watts Australia
14 Mars Road
Lane Cove
NSW 2066

ISBN: 0 7496 3534 7

A CIP catalogue record for this book is available from
the British Library.

Dewey Decimal Classification Number: 629.22

10 9 8 7 6 5 4 3 2 1

Series editor: Sarah Ridley

Printed in Great Britain

Henry Ford

In 1832, William Ford moved
from Ireland to start a new life
in the United States of America.
He bought a farm and married
a woman called Mary Litogot.
In 1863 they had a son, Henry.

Henry was lazy at school and no good at ordinary lessons but he invented a secret alphabet. The teacher couldn't read the notes he passed to his friends!

Henry liked living in the country, but he hated working on the farm.

5

It was how things worked that really fascinated Henry.

One day he decided to find out what would happen if he plugged the spout of the kettle to stop the steam escaping.

He soon got his answer – with a bang!

This didn't stop him from experimenting. He dammed a stream and used the water to power a stone-grinding machine.

Then clocks and clockwork toys caught Henry's interest. He would take them apart to mend them, or just to see how they worked. He couldn't always put them back together.

Henry would often walk for half a day just to be able to look at watchmaker's tools in the city shops. Only Henry's mother believed in his talent.

9

One day Henry saw a steam engine moving under its own power. It was the first vehicle he had seen that didn't use horses to pull it. He stopped it and

asked the driver to show him how it worked. Henry saw that machines like this might replace horses one day.

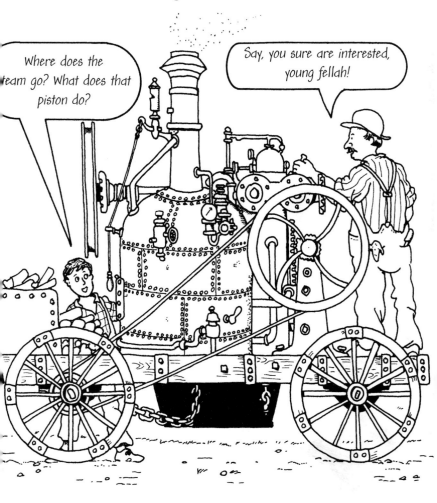

When Henry was thirteen, his mother died. He missed her badly and cut himself off from his family. He preferred to spend hours at his workbench.

While he worked on the farm,
Henry dreamed of building
machines. Maybe some of them
could do the farm work for him.

At the age of seventeen, Henry
decided he couldn't bear life
on the farm any longer. So
he hitched a ride to the city
of Detroit.

His first job was in a factory making railway wagons. He soon moved to another firm making machinery.

All the time he was thinking about how to build a car. He believed that the first person to design a good car would grow very rich as many people would want to own cars.

After two years Henry went back to his father's farm, but not as a farmer. He became an engineer and showed people how traction engines worked.

He married his childhood sweetheart, Clara, who had been waiting for him.

In his spare time, he made two small steam engines. One went a metre or two… the other didn't go at all.

17

One day Henry saw a petrol engine driving a machine to fill bottles. He realised that this was the type of engine he needed for his car. It was small, powerful and didn't need a steam boiler.

He rushed home to tell Clara and sketched out his idea on her music.

Henry and Clara moved back to Detroit, where he worked in a power station. In his free time he began to build a petrol car. Other people were also busy designing cars.

Karl Benz
Germany
1885

Armand Peugot
France
1891

Charles u Frank
Duryea
USA
1893

Henry Ford
USA
?
?

Every evening Henry worked on his car in a shed in the back yard. The first time the engine worked was in the kitchen!

He finished the car at two
o'clock one morning. He was so
excited that he decided to take
Clara and Edsel, their baby, for
a ride at once.

21

Over the next few days Henry drove about the streets of Detroit showing off his new car.

Crowds followed him wherever he went.

One morning he ran into a man and knocked him down. This was the first car accident in the United States. Luckily no one was hurt.

The power station where Henry worked was owned by Thomas Edison, the inventor of the light bulb. One day, Henry decided to show Edison a sketch of his car.

Henry sold his first car for $200 and used the money to start his own company.

Other people were also building cars. By 1899 there were 4,000 cars in the USA. Most of these ran on steam or electric power.

Henry's company only made one car. Then it ran out of money.

Henry was worried that he would not be the first to make a popular car. He decided to build a racing car to get publicity. It won its first race.

Next he built a more powerful car that won more races. The name Henry Ford was becoming famous.

Some Detroit businessmen lent Henry the money to start a new company. They used Henry's signature for the company badge.

At first they made four types of car, but Henry disagreed. He wanted to make only one type of cheap car.

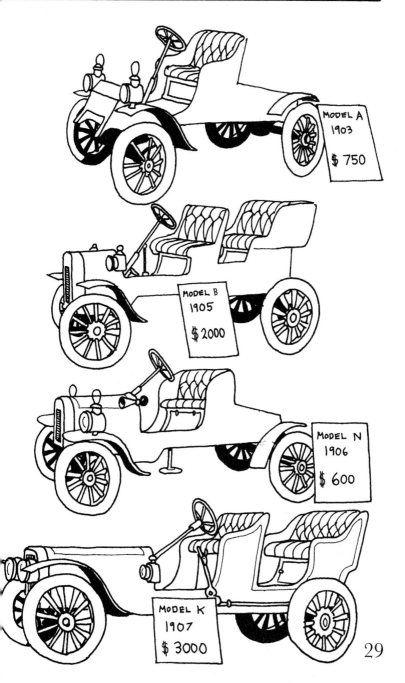

MODEL A
1903

$ 750

MODEL B
1905

$ 2000

MODEL N
1906

$ 600

MODEL K
1907

$ 3000

29

Henry got his way. He designed a car that was cheap, reliable and easy to drive.

The Model-T, or 'Tin Lizzie', was a huge success at once. It was the first car that farmers liked as it was so tough it could manage rough country roads.

The Ford Motor Company built a huge factory called Highland Park. Here thousands of Model-T cars were made using Henry's new idea – the assembly line.

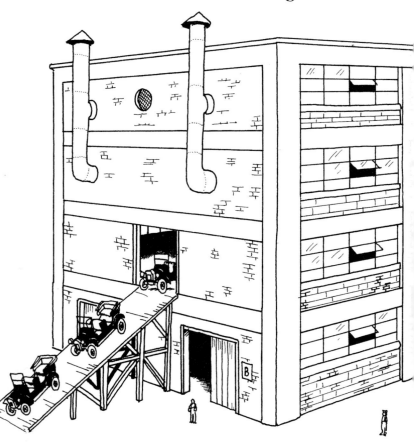

No other company made cars the way the Ford Motor Company did. It was the secret of their success.

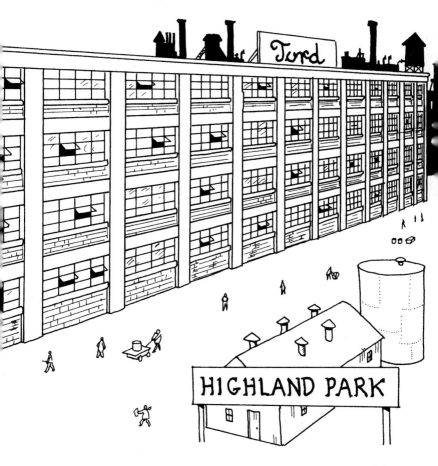

The car travelled on a moving belt, called an assembly line, through the factory. Parts were added until the car was finished.

Each worker had only one task.
All of this made it possible for
Ford cars to be built quickly
and cheaply.

Henry also treated his factory workers better than other factory owners. A welfare department handed out help and advice.

Other workers in the car factories of Detroit earned $2.50 per day. Henry paid his workers $5 per day. Everyone wanted to work for him.

By the 1920s the Model-T car wasn't selling very well. It looked old-fashioned. However, when the factory built a new version without telling him, Henry destroyed the car in a rage.

Eventually, Henry saw that the Model-T had to go. In 1927, the last one was built.

The 'Tin Lizzie' was replaced by the Model-A. It was a huge success, too.

Five years later Henry produced his last car, the V-8.

By now, Henry was the richest and most famous man in America. People wanted to hear his views on everything, but not all Henry's ideas were good. He used his newspaper to spread his opinions.

Henry's ideas became a bit strange. He made his workers eat healthy foods based on soya beans. He taught them country dancing and had the dance steps painted on the floor of a big workshop.

Henry became rather hard on his workers. He wanted to control their lives.

The assembly line went so
fast the workers could hardly
keep up with it.

As Henry grew old he became
more and more confused. He was
very wealthy but spent most of
his time tinkering in his workshop
and reading comics.

At the age of eighty-three,
Henry Ford died. He had
changed the car industry
for ever.

1863 – 1947

More about Henry Ford

Flying Fords

Ford was interested in flying and built three-engined planes which were very modern for the 1920s. One of them was flown to the South Pole.

During the Second World War, he built a huge factory that produced bomber planes on assembly lines, like his cars.

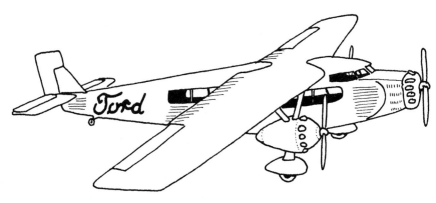

'History is Bunk'

This is one of Henry Ford's most famous remarks. He believed that history that is all about kings and queens is useless. He wanted to show Americans the history of ordinary people and industry. He built Greenfield Village to which he moved the buildings of famous Americans he admired, including Thomas Edison's laboratory. He also built the Henry Ford Museum to house his huge collection of old farm tools, machinery and old-fashioned household goods.

Henry's peace ship

Henry was against war all his life. In 1915, during the First World War, he hired a ship to take him and other leading Americans to Europe to try and stop the fighting. He failed.

Important dates in Henry Ford's lifetime

1863   Henry is born in Michigan, USA.

1880   Henry gets a job as a mechanic.

1888   Henry marries Clara.

1896   Henry builds his first car.

1899   Henry sets up his own company to make cars, but is soon bankrupt.

1901   Henry wins a car race and sets up his second company. It fails too.

1903   Henry builds a new racing car and wins the world record. The Ford Motor Company is founded.

1908   The Model-T car is introduced.

1913   The assembly line is introduced to the Ford Motor Company's factory.

1915   Henry sails to Europe to try and stop the First World War.

1927   The last Model-T car is made.

1928   The first Ford factory opens in England.

1929   The Ford Museum and Greenfield Village is opened.

1947   Henry Ford dies, aged 83.